For the Seniors of 2020

I0159108

written by Manda Lee

ISBN- 13: 978-1-948376-08-2

DNA PUBLISHERS
PO BOX 10391
CORPUS CHRISTI, TX 78460
dnapublishers@yahoo.com

For all the Seniors of 2020

For someone you love

Dedicated to:

_____

_____

_____

_____

_____

_____

_____

~Senior Class of 2020~

You were brought into this world in a very gentle time,
September 11, 2001.
Where we all sheltered in place.
Where we hugged our loved ones tighter.
Where we kept our loved ones closer.
Where we cherished every minute with our families.
Where we were safe at home.

Now, you are a senior in high school. Your biggest accomplishment is walking across the stage on graduation night, but your senior year is now on pause because of COVID-19.

We are keeping our loved ones closer.
We are hugging eachother tighter.
We are cherishing the moments our family
has together.
We are safe at home.
We are united as one.

Your senior memories were put on hold.
Your senior activities were put on hold.
Your prom was put on hold.
Your graduation was put on hold.

Your perseverance was not put on hold.
Your success was not put on hold.
Your future was not put on hold.
You are our future.

You have grown up in a world where we are
reminded by events of the most
important thing in life.
Each other.

Your determination is stronger.
Your love is bold.
You have grown to cherish everyone around you, to believe in your dreams, to embrace the world as it is.
Your light shines brighter.

You will always strive to accomplish your dreams.
You will always adapt to the challenges in life and
overcome them.
You will face the storms head on.
You will embrace your future.

To the Seniors of 2020

The world can learn so much from
you.
Your upbringing influenced who
you are today.
Be proud of who you are and what
you've accomplished.

Keep moving forward.
Keep on smiling.
Cherish every moment.
You will change the world.

www.ingramcontent.com/pod-product-compliance
Lightning Source LLC
Chambersburg PA
CBHW060608030426
42337CB00019B/3676